# About the author

B.L. Matthews is a Maryland poet who has embarked on the journey from her own comfortable boundaries and is now ready to share with the world her experiences. She battles the repercussions of abuse, anxiety, depression and self-doubt and wanted to let those who also live with the beast know that they are not alone. B.L. enjoys a peaceful life with her husband and three children, painting, writing and spending time with their four dogs. She volunteers her time fostering shelter dogs. If she's not with her family, her head is usually buried in a book. She loves to eat MD crabs and play rummy.

'To be a poet, is a condition, not a profession.'
*Robert Graves*

Instagram: @bl.matthews

# COMMITTED

# B.L. MATTHEWS

---

COMMITTED

Vanguard Press

VANGUARD PAPERBACK

© Copyright 2021
**B.L. Matthews**

The right of B.L. Matthews to be identified as author of this work
has been asserted by her in accordance with the
Copyright, Designs and Patents Act 1988.

**All Rights Reserved**

No reproduction, copy or transmission of this publication
may be made without written permission.
No paragraph of this publication may be reproduced,
copied or transmitted save with the written permission of the
publisher, or in accordance with the provisions
of the Copyright Act 1956 (as amended).

Any person who commits any unauthorised act in relation to
this publication may be liable to criminal
prosecution and civil claims for damages.

A CIP catalogue record for this title is
available from the British Library.

ISBN 978 1 80016 047 7

*Vanguard Press is an imprint of
Pegasus Elliot MacKenzie Publishers Ltd.*
www.pegasuspublishers.com

First Published in 2021

**Vanguard Press
Sheraton House Castle Park
Cambridge England**

Printed & Bound in Great Britain

# Dedication

This book is dedicated to my husband, my children and my mom. Thank you for always being the light on my darkest days.

# Acknowledgements

I am forever grateful to my children, Lexi, Matt and Brittnee. I never knew how much of life I wasn't living until you. Thank you for making me a better person. I love you with my whole heart.

To my husband, Rick, for always standing by me and loving me through it all.

To my mom, Brenda, my grandmother, Dixie: you are both my rocks, the sturdiest part of my unsteadiest times.

To my Uncle Nathan, I hope never to be scared of taking a leap of faith, just like you. Thank you for encouraging me to write this book… and doing my illustrations.

To my sister, Brittany, for the times when I had your back and you had mine. I love you.

To my Aunt Rosie, for gifting me her poetic genes.

My love to my friends, for supporting me wholeheartedly.

And lastly, I want to thank you. I hope one day you find the key to unlocking your own peace, even if you must search and unlock it every day. Find your strength to see yourself through… Don't let them win, whoever hurt you.

# Contents

## LUNATIC .................................................. 17

- Anxiety .................................................. 19
- Revenge ................................................. 21
- It was me! .............................................. 23
- Voices .................................................. 24
- Envenom ................................................ 25
- What the dog saw ..................................... 26
- Buried alive ........................................... 29
- Into the fire ........................................... 30
- I don't wear lipstick ................................. 31
- I've gone to find myself ............................ 32
- Wolf ..................................................... 33
- Digging your grave .................................. 37
- Self-destruct .......................................... 38
- Jaded ................................................... 39
- The longer I sit ...................................... 42
- Poison garden ........................................ 45
- Side effects ........................................... 46
- Kisses and curses .................................... 47
- Scorched heart ....................................... 49
- Panic attack .......................................... 50

## DIAGNOSED .................................................................... 53
- Victory or Vice ................................................................ 55
- Scalpel ............................................................................. 57
- Who hurt you? ................................................................ 59
- I'm tired ......................................................................... 61
- Bury the Hatchet ............................................................ 62
- Bandaid .......................................................................... 64
- Fiction ............................................................................ 65
- Damaged ........................................................................ 66
- I need space ................................................................... 67
- Broken ........................................................................... 69
- Flame ............................................................................. 70
- Matter ............................................................................ 71
- Grave ............................................................................. 72
- The weight of regret ...................................................... 73
- I'm fine .......................................................................... 75
- Summer/winter .............................................................. 76
- No longer bleeding ........................................................ 77
- Love the hardest ............................................................ 79
- Where the fireflies die ................................................... 80

## THERAPY ........................................................................ 83
- Clipped Wings ............................................................... 85
- Where I'm meant to be .................................................. 86

| | |
|---|---|
| Chasing | 87 |
| Pick your battles | 88 |
| No easy path | 90 |
| Tell me a lie | 91 |
| Word vomit | 92 |
| Tree | 93 |
| Needle and thread | 94 |
| Hate | 95 |
| Did you see? | 97 |
| She screams in silence | 98 |
| Lotus | 99 |
| Brown eyes | 101 |
| Don't grieve for me | 103 |
| The mirror | 105 |
| Taking on Water | 107 |
| I got your six | 109 |
| My blood | 110 |
| **RECOVERY** | **113** |
| One decision | 115 |
| Your journey | 117 |
| Poppop's little girl | 118 |
| Confident woman | 119 |
| My love | 120 |

Man's world ............................................................ 121
No words ................................................................ 123
Smooth talker ........................................................ 127
Love's spell ............................................................ 128
True story .............................................................. 129
Lullaby ................................................................... 131
Her man ................................................................. 132
Phoenix .................................................................. 133
Hypnotic ................................................................ 136
I need a sinner ....................................................... 137
The cost of time .................................................... 139
All eyes on her ...................................................... 141
Enigma ................................................................... 144
Essence of a storm ................................................ 145
White knight ......................................................... 147

# LUNATIC

*I remained too much inside my head and ended up losing my mind.*
Edgar Allen Poe

# Anxiety

There is a war inside my head,
so terrible and true.
I'd rather crawl back in bed,
than face the day anew.

I'm a slave to my fear of falling;
I'm losing myself in this plight.
I can hear my courage calling
but my confidence can't seem to take flight.

My mind is a bloody battlefield,
where I have fought and lost.
I haven't the strength to pick up my shield.
My sword, my adversary tossed.

I am broken and defeated,
my head too heavy to lift.
My will to fight has retreated,
my soul is set adrift.

I look in my attacker's eyes
and see they are dark blue.
I haven't the strength to rise
and continue this battle through.

Those eyes they match my own,
I have been betrayed.
My brain is no longer my home,
it's not a safe place to stay.

For I know my enemy is ruthless,
to my disappointment and dismay.
To hide or cower would be useless.
I must continue to fight the same monster I lost to today.

# Revenge

The beast that hides in shadows,
always lurking around nearby.
Rib cage jutting from his gut…
lips dusty and bone dry.

There's something to say about one so desperate
to satisfy his needs.
How fascinating it must be
to watch him hunt and feed.

Tonight, the creature is on the prowl;
Crimson revenge he seeks.
To settle this particular score,
pristine in his technique.

He shall feed into his hunger.
His persistence breaks his chains.
For God so help the deserving soul
that is the target of his rage.

# It was me!

If reincarnation were true,
I wish you came back as a bee.
You'd die after picking just one victim
and never hurt anybody but me.

An injured coyote on the trail,
I wish you came back as.
When the snow-covered path proved to be too much,
the pack would consume your carcass.

A praying mantis on the window
is what you should be next.
After your lady mates with you,
you'd wish you'd never had sex.

A silver krill in the ocean blue,
what a great match you would make.
When the whale is ready to feed
all your little bones he'll break.

A field mouse sitting on a stump,
I'm sure that you could be.
And when the eagle swoops down from above,
I want you to know it was me!

# Voices

*Are you good enough?*
*Did you do your best?*
*Keep pressing and pushing*
*you don't deserve rest.*

To be a good person
you must show support.
No time for yourself,
else your expectations fall short.

I listen to the voices,
talking me through…
*I know you're exhausted*
*but you've got more to do.*

Now put on your make up
and get out of bed.
*No time for rest,*
*you'll do that when you're dead.*

Although my own thoughts
have me fully engrossed.
It's the voices outside my head
that bother me most.

# Envenom

My brain is lying to me,
sending bad thoughts through my memory.
Why can't my insights be rainbows and stars?
Instead they're woven with fear and scars...

Places I wish I'd never go,
my mind sends me through
ever so slow...
Slowly, so I have time to
absorb
all these abandoned feelings
I want to abort.

Why is my brain constantly
bullying me?
It's unfair because no one
else can see.
It pours me a cup of black toxic liquid.
At first, I refused but now I'm addicted.

It's poisoning the healthy stems of my brain,
tricking me to cry out when there is no real pain.
My cerebrum it flows forcefully throughout.
Rotting the good, the bad it draws out.

Dizzying toxins like littering debris,
this poison I drink will be the death of me.

# What the dog saw

You came home loaded;
Once again, I was your target.
Praying you'd pass out soon,
in the morning you'd forget.

This time was different
than all the times before.
You smelled of resentment
when you swayed through the door.

Your anger had no reason;
You were hateful just because.
And I the willing victim…
A martyr to your cause.

Our children fast asleep
as you stumbled your way to the steps.
Too scared that you'd hurt them,
a mother would go to great depths.

The day finally came
where you stepped over the line
and I finally fought back,
no longer the victim to your crime.

If time I could rewind,
I wouldn't change anything at all.
I have absolutely no regrets,
not a single salty tear to fall.

The only witness to your violence
stood silent against the wall.
No one would ever believe my plea
but our dog had seen it all.

She was there when I was broken
and when I rose above it all.
If only I was able to prove
what only the dog saw.

# Buried alive

My oxygen's depleting;
I'm scarcely alive.
I've locked myself inside this tomb...
please don't let me die.

I craved isolation;
So I crawled inside my mind.
Buried myself so deep inside
where nobody could find.

The walls are caving in on me;
The coffin lid slammed tight.
I scratched and screamed for hours
but no one could hear my fight.

I'm a victim to my mind,
the predator and the prey.
It slowly devours me alive,
while everyone looks away.

# Into the fire

I jumped feet first into the fire
and arose from the flames a stronger version of myself.
I mastered the hot coals,
my feet consumed in angry blue flame
but I can no longer feel the agony
of each blistered step.
My lungs use to expel black soot.
Now I breathe deeply
the sweet carbon poisoning of her flames.
My skin would crawl inside itself.
Now I ignite flames from
my very own pores.
My tongue is a match
and with one flick
I spit fire.
I spent night after night
being digested by this
monstrous beauty that
I simply
became
her
to
survive.

# I don't wear lipstick

Today's the big day,
dressed to the nines.
I knew this day would come
but not so quickly in time.

All of my family will be there,
my closest friends too.
I'll be so happy to celebrate
and spend this time with you.

I'm in my favorite outfit,
picked out my matching shoes.
But for my necklace and earrings,
I wonder which to choose.

My skin is turning blue.
So, they layer my make-up thick…
I hope the mortician knows
that I don't wear lipstick.

# I've gone to find myself

Don't knock on my door
there's no one home.
I've gone to find myself
cause I'm scared to be alone.

My anxiety overly warning me
of constant impending doom.
My thoughts are my mausoleum,
my brain is the tomb.

I'm out of my mind
but I don't know where I went.
Over a lifetime of worry…
Will I ever be content?

My heart breaks up
as my brain breaks down.
I've searched high and low,
still no sanity to be found.

If you wish to pay me a visit,
understand I'm missing throughout.
For my body may have me checked in
but my mind has me checked out.

# Wolf

It's my agonizing battle
every single night.
Keep the wolf from violating my brain
until the moon becomes daylight.

I've sworn to protect my psyche
and not let the crazed wolf near.
But if the beast is victorious,
it's my mind I'll lose, I fear.

The wolf is a figment;
My secret feelings of dread.
It appears he'll give me no peace
until the day I'm dead.

He cleverly creeps up behind me,
always when he's least expected.
Like anxiety looming in my mind,
I simply can't detect it.

I fight this battle daily
with the weapons I have brought.
But it seems never ending.
I'm helplessly distraught.

There's a good chance I'll lose this battle
and he'll triumphantly win.
So why do I bother fighting
when I can simply let him in?

# Digging your grave

The weight you've made me carry,
rests heavy on my shoulders.
The words you said festered in my head
and crushed my heart like a boulder.

You'll never hurt anyone again,
this much I know is true.
I was told to handle my own
and that's exactly what I'll do.

I sift the dirt through my fingers,
as I sit here and wonder why.
Why do you make me do these things?
I've cried till my tears are dry.

My shovel's getting heavy,
as I toss the dirt to the side.
I've carried your body from there to here,
in the field where I hide my crime.

A chilly six feet under
is where your rotting body will be.
You may lie, cheat, beg and steal
but you'll never again lay a hand on me.

# Self-destruct

I'm hardwired like a robot,
Programmed for a mission.
Finger on the button;
Key in the ignition.

Too many demands,
my motherboard can't decipher.
Shooting off red flags…
I may need rewired.

My brain is the screen;
static is on display.
I've tried to reboot,
but all I do is replay.

My power is corroded,
my memory all but done.
The error on my screen reads:
Self-destruct in…
5
4
3
2
1

# Jaded

My dear, please take the time and I'll fill you in,
on how the tailoring of my thoughts begin.

You see, I was not merely put on this earth
to loathe your being, thus question my worth.

Deep within me is a maniacal monstrosity,
built with an unmeasurable velocity.

The calculation of my thinking and quick wit,
unstoppable like the pendulum and the pit.

So please believe me when I insist,
you must visit a proctologist.

To dislodge your cranium from your rectum,
'twas propelled inward with quite a momentum.

It's unfathomable to rightly conceive
that you've convinced the masses to believe.

You've got all their best interests at heart.
People are stupid, but a person is smart.

I sat back studying all your tactics,
memorized your maneuvers and dynamics.

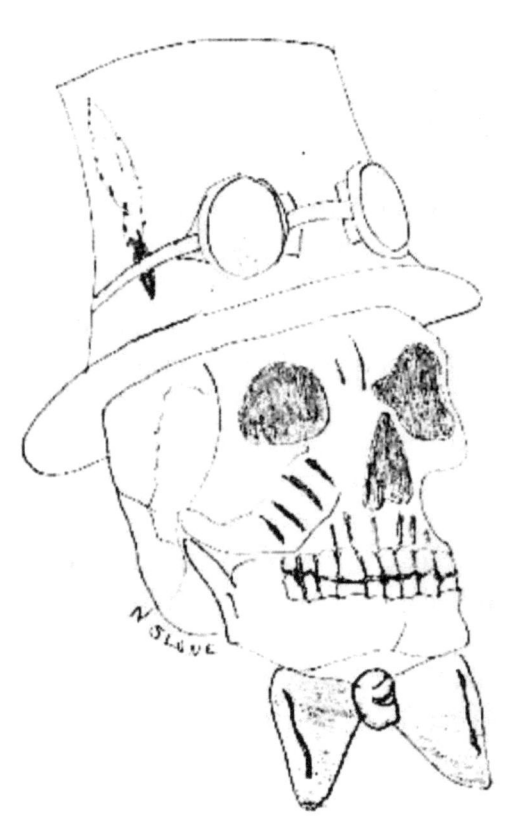

They celebrated you with agnosy and ignorance,
defended your purposes with such belligerence.

The time thus came for me to expose
the wicked demon you are from head to toe.

No one believed me so I was mocked.
Scorned to this day, sickened with shock.

Their feeble minds you've unnaturally invaded
but don't listen to me, I'm just bitterly jaded.

# The longer I sit

I pay for my life
with pieces of my dreams…
The longer I sit,
the further away they seem.

There's always a rush
to try and grow up,
and then once you do,
you know you've messed up.

At one point you thought
the world was all yours,
and adventure awaited
behind all closed doors.

But now you find
the doors just stay closed…
Everyone guesses
and nobody knows.

Your dreams were planted
to make you feel small,
and rarely a seed
stems from them at all.

For life crashes into you,
all at full force.
My car's in the race…
but it's been run off course.

Now all my aspirations
are nothing but daydreams.
The longer I sit…
the further away they seem.

# Poison garden

My thoughts are a poison garden…
the seeds I've sown myself.
Tread carefully where you travel,
I can't be responsible for your health.

First grown is the ivy,
its vines a beauty divine.
Venomous leaves prey on my skin…
My psyche has inevitably declined.

Nightshade coils around my brain,
its solanine poisoning my dreams.
Rapids flowing like toxic streams,
nothing is actually as it seems.

Hemlock grows so bountiful.
What a tricky beauty throughout.
Do you trust her lovely flowers?
I advise, you must look out.

My garden is flourishing with madness;
Where beauty appears to display.
My mind the starving predator
and I… its only prey.

# Side effects

These walls I've built;
My anxious brain.
The constant guilt;
The unstoppable pain.

Countless side effects
from years of abuse.
Counseling, medication
proved no use.

I paid your debt
with thousands of tears.
Regret and resentment
built up for years.

The devil's right hand,
have you no shame?
But why the hell should you
when you're never to blame.

# Kisses and curses

I listened as the hisses
spewed from your lips.
Can you ever tell the truth?
Do you know that it exists?

The wrongs that you have done…
will forever and always be.
They've defined who you are;
All the lies that you told me.

You know that I know
but not so much.
My stomach violently convulses
with your every little touch.

Your scales slither on my skin,
your forked tongue in my ear.
Years of constant neglect
has left me with no fear.

I kissed you goodnight
knowing all that you have done.
Damning you with curses for
the lies that you have spun.

I'll fix this come morning…
no sooner can I wait.
Ready to live with love in my heart
no longer consumed by hate.

# Scorched heart

I've scorched my heart
while trying to put out your fire.
Now that I'm consumed in your flames
suddenly you're nowhere to be seen.

# Panic attack

Suffocating I sit in silence…
The noises are so loud.
I pressed my feverish brow
to the solid cold ground.

The walls are caving in around me,
I see no way out.
I'm panicking on the inside;
I've lost myself in doubt.

Hurry please come find me,
I feel like I'm passing out.
My heart beats a thousand beats…
No voice for me to shout.

The shaking is relentless.
I'm paralyzed in fear.
I'm at my mind's mercy,
darkness is looming near.

I'm all alone and I can't breathe;
I'm drowning in my worries.
I take water in, as I sink within;
My vision has gone blurry.

Don't feel sorry for me.
This is my cross to bear.
My wars are within, I don't always win
as you live your life unaware.

# DIAGNOSED

*You can't go back and change the beginning, but you can start where you are and change the ending.*

C.S. Lewis

# Victory or Vice

Wake up, rollover,
lying in bed.
"Today should be easier,"
to myself, I said.

Weary eyes half closed,
another sleepless night.
What's today's fate,
Victory or Vice?

Some days are solid,
bravery from the start.
Other days I'm certain
I'm slowly falling apart.

My victory days,
I'm cunning and clever.
Ready to take on the world
And all its endeavors.

Vice, I'm paranoid,
shaky and sick.
Welcoming the lock up
like a lunatic.

Which one do I get?
Only fate can tell.
My illness is a curse,
sent straight from hell.

# Scalpel

I saw the shiny blade
that glinted in the light.
Across the room…
On a sanitized tray.
Calling to me…
Taunting me….
I took the scalpel
and very carefully,
very cautiously,
started to carve out my heart.
Feverishly cutting
to release the grenade within.
The promise of an untimely explosion.
The pain of letting it go weighed less
then the pain of keeping it.
Besides, it's no longer mine.
It belongs to someone who will handle it
more delicately than I.

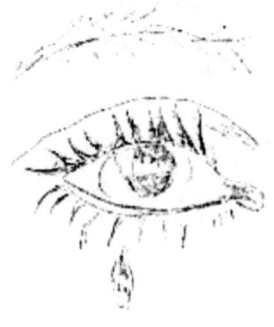

N SLONG

# Who hurt you?

I can see you're trying your best to be tough
a façade you display 'cause you've had enough.

You act so guarded,
        nervous,
        unsure.
Finding self-love is a misguided lure.

You present yourself for the world to see.
You've got it all together,
        established,
        carefree.

But once you're home and you remove your mask;
Being friendly and social, an impossible task.

You are not nearly as hard as you seem;
Putting up a front is part of your scheme.

Deep down inside your lonely heart is aching.
Falling in love is a chance not worth taking.

So, you live every day the same as the last;
Wake up each morning and put on your mask.

Because what kind of pain would you be willing to feel?
If you showed you were genuine and real.

Instead you act as if you haven't a soul to care.
And let someone cross you if they dare.

I watch you struggle with this every day,
I know the truth but I won't say.

I hope one day you let your feelings push through.
Don't let them win… whoever hurt you.

# I'm tired

All of the people that I cannot please,
are drawn to me like a contagious disease.

I am but simply one person alone;
Take my atoms and make my clone.

For I am at my own wits' end;
promises kept, good deeds I intend.

My generosity's milk has long been expired…
I do my best, but damn I'm tired.

# Bury the Hatchet

Bury the hatchet
with memories I shouldn't keep,
But it seems that every night
I excavate them in my sleep.

You see, when I am cognoscente
I have all the control,
and seldom let a painful thought
ever touch my soul.

But it's at night when I lay down
and on the pillow my head does rest;
That all these vivid living nightmares
put my resolve up to the test.

I do not want to close my eyes,
I'll have more dreams, I fear…
and all my grisly premonitions
will be lurking somewhere near.

My head is getting heavy;
I know I'll lose this fight.
To dream all those odious dreams
because what's wrong never becomes right.

My demons won't sleep,
though many years I've tried;
I took the pills and prayed the prayers
but it appears that someone lied.

Because I was never granted solace
And on my knees, I've cried;
Begging for self-forgiveness,
I swallowed that pill called pride.

Now my mind's reel keeps turning
with all of my regrets,
and I'm still in mourning…
for a forgiveness I won't let myself get.

# Bandaid

Skin colored so as to mask
the healing process of
what's happening underneath.
A genesis of new cells
to formulate new life,
blood pumping,
new flesh regenerating.
All of these processes
in place for a simple scratch…
Can you imagine what goes into
healing a broken heart?

# Fiction

I bury my head in a book because I crave the adventure
I'm not brave enough to seek.

# Damaged

Damaged doesn't mean delicate,
don't let your prejudice deceive.
Her skin was thickened by insensitive blows…
she's withstood what most couldn't conceive.

# I need space

The days when you want to lay in bed and melt away.
Your phone starts to ring but you have nothing to say.

Stand in the shower let the water caress your face…
Spending some time alone because you simply need space.

Take your morning pill, to keep your depression in check…
Heart behind the wheel, head is a wreck.

You've checked out of the resort called reality.
Just for today you're hiding like an escapee.

You've silenced your mouth but your mind is a riot.
Only those who love you can hear when you're quiet.

# Broken

I thought I was unbreakable,
I was wrong.
I was broken badly,
    repeatedly.
When I was put back together
    I was weaker,
    more dependent,
    fragile.
I was placed on such a delicate pedestal
in such a high tower.
Just when I started to have faith in the stability
of the pedestal,
it's pushed from beneath my feet.
The only person to catch me
was the same monster
who wished me harm on my fall.
Punished for questioning the lies,
trying to find the truth.
I kept falling from this high tower over and over.
Until one day I caught myself…

AND EVERYTHING CHANGED.

# Flame

A flame of anger fills your heart throughout,
pointing your finger at everyone for blame.
The pain you impose on others due to self-doubt,
it's so easy for you to turn your rage out
because a candle can't get burned by its own flame.

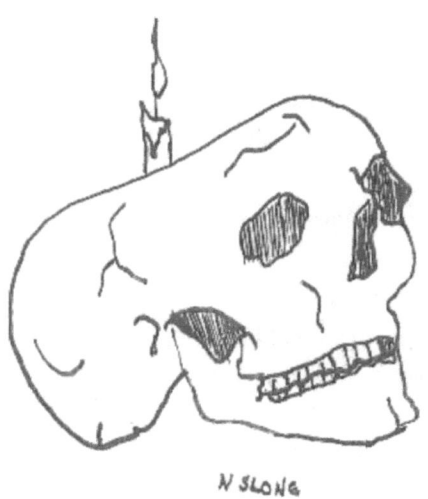

# Matter

Mind over matter,
at least that's what they say.
Except when the matter is your mind
and you're consumed every day.

# Grave

I dug a grave for you in my heart
and that is where you'll stay.
Dead and buried like other useless things
that simply won't decay.

# The weight of regret

Vast scales on my heart,
weighing out of sync.
I don't deserve all the punishment
that I have grown to think.

Heavy emotions on my mind,
to forgive myself I couldn't.
Others I would have spared.
Yet, I punish myself to the fullest.

My mind a broken record…
The tune it plays, the past.
Healing comes in stages…
nor does it ever last.

My misfortunes I keep for solace,
locked away in my mind's cage.
My regrets replay their performance…
My tears have become their stage.

# I'm fine

When asked if she's all right,
She says "I'm fine".
Desperately waiting for that one person
who won't believe her.

# Summer/winter

You are my summer,
so inviting and warm.
I am your winter,
an emotional storm.

Your summer is soothing,
a calm gentle breeze.
My winter is challenging,
a gnawing unease.

Why do you stay so long in my cold?
What makes you so stubbornly bold?

I am the queen of my glacial castle.
But just like the ice, I'm see through and fragile.
I sit here alone, on my frozen throne.
As the snow falls quietly and the winds furiously moan.

My darkest secrets you seem to know…
maybe that's why you stay and not go.

# No longer bleeding

My wounds no longer bleed
but they still cause pain.
Daily battles within
leave me battered and drained.

Remnants of a past
I will never fully forgive.
Prospects of a life
I will never fully live.

I am too scared
to make one mistake.
The times I was thoughtless
have shocked me awake.

Be careful with me
I've buried my demons down deep.
Trust me, they're not dead;
They've simply gone to sleep.

# Love the hardest

When the day isn't going the best
and in my attempts to turn it around I fail.
I succumb to the disappointment and anger,
like a wild rose being beaten by a storm,
my petals have fallen.
My beauty no longer robust.
I may appear I want to be left alone
but nothing could be a greater lie.
I desperately yearn for solace.
I need you to run your fingers across my thorns
knowing they will cut you.
You'll bleed with every touch while consoling me
but this is when I need you to love me the hardest.
Tomorrow I will drink from my roots and try to replenish
but today I need you to just hug me and all my thorns.

# Where the fireflies die

The imagination of a child,
mesmerized by the world still anew.
Every bee, every flower, every puddle
is fascinating.
Everything is seen in bright colors,
chasing butterflies in the fields.
Hold on to that wonder;
Keep a tight grasp on to that world of innocence.
Otherwise you must grow up and bury all those dreams
where the fireflies die.

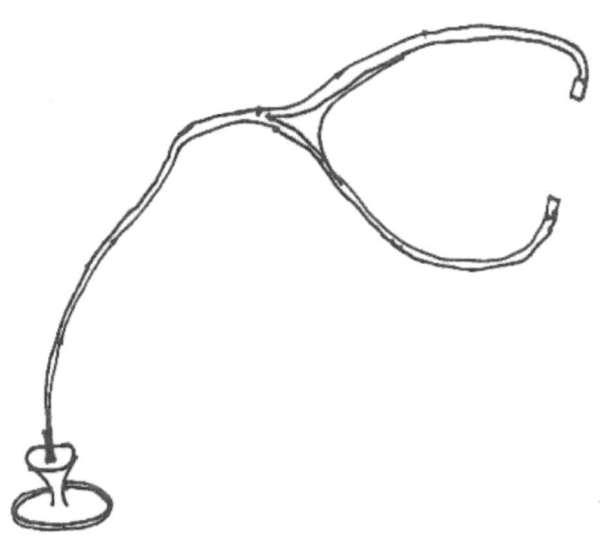

# THERAPY

*I stopped waiting for the light at the end of the tunnel
and lit that bitch myself.*

Anonymous

# Clipped Wings

You can tear apart my sense of self,
rip my confidence from my soul.
Laugh at me while I compose myself,
thinking that my voice you stole.

You may have torn me violently from the sky
and clipped both of my beautiful wings.
I take flight within and rise in victory
because an injured bird still sings.

# Where I'm meant to be

I am not meant to be where I am,
but I can't get to where I'm meant to be.
I can feel it deep within my bones,
my soul slowly dying to be set free.

My life is but only half complete,
as I know my family is whole;
But this place where I am currently at
I desperately loathe with all my soul.

I know I have a greater purpose
it's longing to be applied;
But I can't seem to get out from where I'm at,
for many years I've tried.

Sadly, I'm stuck in life's violent quicksand
with no escape that can be seen.
I am not meant to be where I am,
but I can't get to where I'm meant to be.

# Chasing

The minute things slow down I start to panic.
What is life, if not constantly chasing after
something… anything?
The slowness leaves me in fear
that I reached the pinnacle
and I've nothing left to gain
but a peaceful death.

# Pick your battles

If everything that doesn't go your way
always turns into a fight,
and you've terminated friendships
just to prove that you are right.

If you get pleasure seeking revenge
and hurting your enemies out of spite.
If every little mole hill
turns into mountain overnight.

To the friends you have remaining,
how draining it must be.
You may find they no longer respond
to your negativity.

Every time someone talks to you
your mood is always down.
You'll drown in your own misery,
if you don't turn things around.

Try to relax and live your life
slowly day by day.
You won't win at playing this game
if you always get your way.

Some days will be good, others bad.
You must learn to bend with the breeze…
else you'll spend your whole life fighting
and never be at ease.

# No easy path

Life has a way of testing us,
though no restraint it shows.
Putting us through unimaginable suffering
from the knives it deliberately throws.

If not quick from the start, it'll pierce your heart…
As it perforates your tender skin.
Life's wrath digest, your brave quest…
searching for the warrior within.

Like a pan to the fire, life's pure desire…
begging you to give in.
Esteem dying, moral compromising…
in life's ocean, sink or swim.

We each travel through myriads
of trials and tribulations.
When you've completed your quest and done your best,
You'll know you've reached your destination.

# Tell me a lie

Tell me a lie, so that I may believe it.
Tell me another, so that I am convinced of its truth.
The fragile story you tell,
with so many cracks in its foundation
is not sturdy.
The higher you build your castle of lies,
the harder it will hurt
when it all comes crashing down.

# Word vomit

I've got too much to say.
I must get it all out.
It's better draining from my pen
than hearing it from my mouth.

I'm usually pretty quiet,
but thoughts I wouldn't normally speak.
Come flowing onto paper
like a leaky kitchen sink.

Keeping all this in
would be detrimental to my health.
Like an addict needing more
but lacking the financial wealth.

Writing is my outlet.
The best form of therapy.
It's my drug of choice,
gives me clarity.

Instead of speaking
I'll let my opinions seep in.
My words bleed onto the paper;
My blood flows through the pen.

# Tree

I fancy myself to be like a tree;
Bending with life's winds with the greatest of ease.
Relying on my roots to hold me down.
I wear my leaves like an emerald crown.

I take mercy on the many critters of the land;
When they need refuge, I hold out my hand.
The sun bakes me like an apple pie…
Giving me the nourishment needed to survive.

Winters come and summers go,
that icy chill has started to blow.
I shed all my leaves on the frozen floor;
Watch them all perish as they have before.

The birds have all but disappeared.
The next big freeze is coming near.
I sink into a death-like slumber,
waking up next spring with an insatiable hunger.

There's still something I'm aching to know,
why must I die inside to be able to grow?

# Needle and thread

My lips are sewn shut
with every word I never said.
Swallowed down deep inside,
each word has formed the thread.

My tongue molded the needle,
though it never did its part.
Stabbed through my lips of unspoken words;
Felt through my chastised heart.

# Hate

Have you ever hated someone so much for doing you wrong...
Even though you knew better than to get involved all along?
Do you despise the way they look, they smile, they walk...
Even cringe a bit when they open their mouths to talk?
How have you allowed them to hurt you so,
to where your heart is unable to let go.
Were you the only person in their path
or were your friends and family part of their wrath?
The hate you've built up is like a demon's seed.
Growing in your mind, invading like a weed.
Before you know it you're completely consumed,
all future memories unfortunately doomed.
At this point you've given them all the power,
forbidding yourself to heal has made you sour.
You enact a plan to make them pay for their troubles.
You're furious when you notice they take pleasure in your struggles.
The subsequent theory that I've come upon;
to have the ultimate revenge you must simply move on.

# Did you see?

When you looked in my eyes…
Did you see
a sea of hopelessness?
A fisherman caught
in a hurricane?
Did you see me
holding my own head
under those waters,
only allowing myself
enough air to sustain life?
The twisting, shaking,
earth shattering pieces
of my memories pushing forward.
Did you see the betrayal of my soul?
The way it tries to rip
apart from my heart?
…Did you like it?

# She screams in silence

She wondered if she was that transparent.
Like an ant through a looking glass,
while the sun is at the perfect angle.
The world so big,
        so mean,
                so greedy.
And yet she,
        so small
                and swallowable.
Gobbled up by the bustling world around her.
Everyone doing busy things.
Could she simply melt into the background
and just exist?
Must she take her place amongst the masses
and make like a good little girl?
Or does she make herself known?
Make her mark on a world that
is not yet ready for her?

# Lotus

Once just a seed set away on a breeze,
determined to take root before the first freeze.

Nature wasn't kind to make the landing easy.
Into the mud, the seed plummeted deeply.

Despair and dismay could have overtaken
but the seed's determination was not easily shaken.

Through the mud it viewed a promising start
and pushed and pushed with all its heart.

To penetrate the murky surface far above,
sunlight and vitamins the seed was bereft of.

Through the cold dark swamp, it grew and flourished.
Made the best of its post and magically self-nourished.

The lotus, unbreakable now with a stem long and strong.
Grew with splendor and beauty that was there all along.

So, when you find yourself stuck in the mud…
the world's negativity beginning to flood.

Think of the lotus and find the strength from within…
because trials and struggles will come to an end.

# Brown eyes

So much of life is already gone;
Lessons learned and then moved on.

From a past of abuse, fleeing from sorrow;
To the hope of sunlight seen in tomorrow.

Her heart has hurt, her eyes have cried,
she's believed in the truth and then in lies.

She will not break but always bends,
like a river flowing that never ends.

She's seen pain in leaps and bounds,
her heart left broken on the ground.

So much of herself she chooses to give,
leaves not much left for her to live.

She covers the pain in her best disguise.
What is she hiding behind those brown eyes?

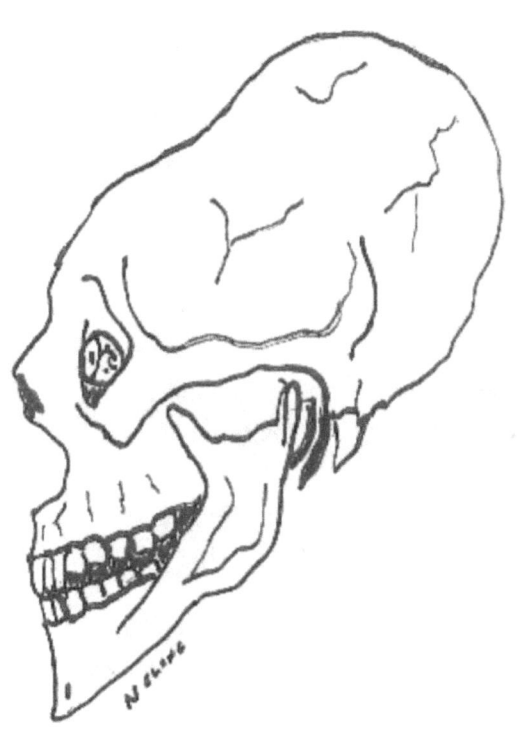

# Don't grieve for me

Don't grieve for me.
Don't pretend that you care.
When the reaper comes calling,
I don't want you there.

Please spare my soul
your cheap parlor tricks.
The show you've put on
is straight politics.

Don't come to my casket.
Don't cry out my name.
Instead kindly stay home
and drown in your shame.

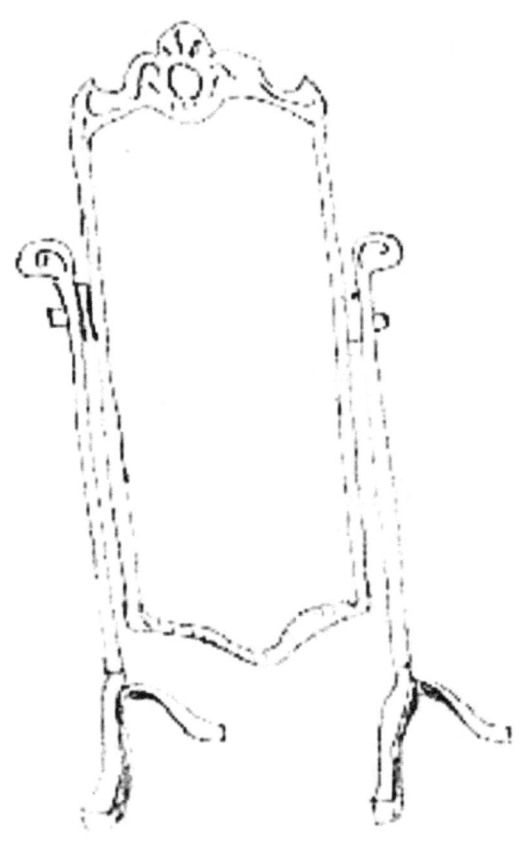

# The mirror

She has the fire of a dragon
with tenacity to spare…
The electricity of an eel,
test her if you dare.

Standing strong for her convictions;
She would never do anyone harm.
When the nay-sayers contended with her,
she'd convince them with her charm.

Wholeheartedly I wished to be her,
so I shadowed my behavior in her grace.
Time again I'd prove myself,
a gentle warrior to not be replaced.

I'd bravely protect the ones I loved
for so long as I possibly could.
I'd spread my hand all over the land
by doing all that is good.

One day I went to find her,
where I often saw her before.
Shattered and broken in my dressing room
was my mirror laying on the floor.

It took my breath to recognize;
I couldn't conceive what I saw.
I was looking at my own reflection
wishing to be me all along.

# Taking on Water

The ship is slowly drowning
in a black sea of despair.
Alone in the murky waters
without a hope or prayer.

She weathered a violent storm
and although she did fight…
day after day she was beaten down
without an end in sight.

Each day she strived her hardest
to try and stay adrift.
Piece by piece she fell apart
into the ocean so swift.

Her spirit still sustaining
and wanted to navigate on.
But the weight was too much to bear…
heavy with the water it had taken on.

The ship had only one choice
in her doomed state of being.
Hope that someone sees her struggles
but help could nowhere be seen.

Into the dark she started to sink,
The sea was swallowing whole.
The depths may steal this vessel
but it will never take her soul.

This ship I could relate,
some many years ago.
Feelings of despair and abandonment
I couldn't comprehend let go.

You can fight to stay alive.
I know, I've been there too.
And if your ship can't find the light,
I'll sit in the dark with you.

# I got your six

This thing that you are fighting,
you don't have to do it alone.
I'm here whenever you need me,
please just pick up the phone.

Secretly you might be scared,
but keep your chin held high.
Bravery is birthed from fear…
You can defeat this if you try.

You've got the power inside you.
You have a strength you never knew.
And if mistakes are all you make,
just know that I got you.

# My blood

I've seen you on your bad days,
withdrawing from the drugs.
I've wrapped you in my arms,
in a warm and loving hug.

I know that's not nearly enough…
you're fighting this battle on your own.
I can be here to support you
but ultimately you must do it alone.

The shaking, the sickness
the vomit and sweat.
You dropped your quarter in the slot
when you never should have bet.

Now here I sit beside you,
running my hand across your back.
As you violently expel the poisons
that have had you under attack.

You must find the will within
and want to make a clean new start.
Because every day that you're addicted
you're breaking somebody's heart.

I can't comprehend infecting my body
with all the venom you do.
But, no matter how much you harm yourself,
Please remember I'll always love you.

# RECOVERY

*This above all; To thine own self be true.*

William Shakespeare

# One decision

Who would you have been
if you made a different choice,
took a different path,
heeded a different voice?

Decisions are the maps
to our future my friend…
Where one road begins
another ends.

Our destiny's web
of splintered quests.
Intertwined together
like vines compressed.

Would your life have changed
its billowing flow,
if you wanted to say yes…
but instead said no?

Would you still be where
you are today
or would your life have
turned out a different way?

We are but one
decision more,
from closing one window
thus, opening a new door.

# Your journey

Thoughts aren't real until they are spoken;
a wedding ring holds no magic, but it's still a token.
Feelings aren't true until they manifest;
your journey is your very own spiraling quest.

You can't walk in snow without making prints;
You'll always have germs no matter how much you rinse.
No two people will ever think the same;
A rainbow won't appear without a little rain.

You don't get bitter by not getting hurt;
Your feet will never step twice in the exact same dirt.
Thoughts, moments and memories will always live on;
Master your future, sing your own song.

# Poppop's little girl

If you were still alive…
what would you look at me and see?
Would you be proud that I turned out to be,
all you'd hoped I'd be?

Would you make me feel safe,
like poppops always do?
Would you tell me I'm grandpop's girl
and whisper "I love you."

I crave to know what I have missed
in all these passing years.
Would you have told the boys to stay away
and wiped away my tears?

I was told you asked to see me
on the hospital bed where you laid.
The nurses snuck me in to say goodbye
On that sad and mournful day.

I've missed your stories and playfulness,
with my heart I wish you could've stayed.
I'm eager to catch up on lost time,
when we meet again someday.

# Confident woman

Alarm goes off;
Roll out of bed.
Eyeliner penciled in;
Lipstick bright red.

Confident smile;
Hips that twitch.
I am a sexy bold beautiful witch.

Curse you I may;
Worship me you might.
I am a mermaid by day and a siren at night

To cross me is brave;
I do not forgive.
Depending on your sin, you may not live.

I have ice in my veins and fire in my soul.
My vengeance is fearful, frightening, and bold.

I am a confident woman, dare I say.
Wanna have fun?
I'll show you the way.

# My love

You are where my mind goes
when it searches for peace.
My chemical balance…
You calm my chaos
and sing my demons to sleep.

# Man's world

You say feminist in a
condescending way.
Like it's a dirty word
for only bitches to say.

Sadly, women have been
the last to receive rights.
For every step forward,
we've had to fight.

Women are rising up
and realizing our worth.
Tearing down ancient stigmas,
making our mark on this earth.

Speaking up for ourselves,
as well as for others.
We are raising our daughters to be strong,
building off the strength of our mothers.

Our shoulders are solid,
we've carried heavy burdens.
That would have broken the backs
of your strongest men for certain.

We didn't need you
to get where we are.
We've done it without a man's help
thus far.

Times will change,
we just don't know when.
Because who wants to live
in a man's world but men?

# No words

Words mean nothing
dare I say.
I love yous are spoken falsely
every single day.

Show me who you are,
words can be such lies.
Actions speak louder
and need no alibis.

A kiss goodbye,
a hug warm and loving,
drive safely my dear,
tissues for a nose that's running.

Cooking dinner at night,
a kiss on the cheek,
a smile as you walk by,
a wink when you speak.

Express to me
just how you feel.
It's more welcomed,
genuine and real.

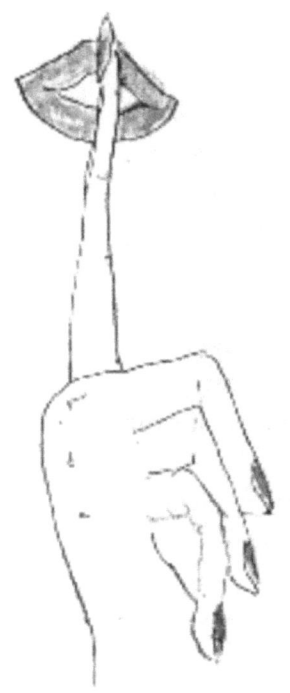

Show me who you are,
words are not believed.
Actions are clearer,
Can't be deceived.

Talk no more,
show me love instead.
Drink in the sweet honey,
no words need to be said.

# Smooth talker

Oh yeah, smooth talker,
I know your type.
Gentlemen by day,
player by night.

Prowling the options
of tonight's main dish,
adjusting your tie,
selecting your pick.

Which lucky lady
will be yours at dusk?
Whisked away to your bed
of mahogany and musk.

You better seal the deal
before your vanity fades.
Will you choose the Queen of Hearts
or the Ace of Spades?

Women are dangerous
when love's at stake.
Don't play with her heart,
it's not a toy to break.

# Love's spell

What spell did you cast on the roses
to make them rejoice from above?
And for fragrance sake, smell so divine
as to make one fall in love?

Scarlet as one's own blood.
A token of the heart
and when love has run its course,
its leaves to pick apart.

A symbol of loyalty,
unless otherwise implied.
'Tis such a precious gift,
unless it was denied.

# True story

Listen up, I'll tell you a story.
A story of times before.
When an unlikely couple met
and the stork left me at their door.

My parents were an odd pair,
as odd pairs came to be.
They were never meant to happen;
but despite all that, bore me.

My mother an unsuspecting angel
who oozed love from her pores.
My father, an evil demon seed…
a womanizing, man whore.

My mother true in nature,
was otherwise content.
Went searching for trouble
and damn if she didn't find it.

My father, that selfish bastard,
would other women please.
Leaving my mother wounded
and crying on her knees.

She noticed one day in disbelief
her body had started to change.
She smiled rubbing her growing belly
though all her energy drained.

"You're not keeping that baby,"
he said, with venom in his voice.
Sat my mother down and
demanded she make a choice.

My mother knew with all her heart
a mother she wanted to be.
Despite her loving this evil man,
she knew she wanted to keep me.

Well, I am here and he is not...
So I guess we see who won.
Innocence took the victory this time,
you ignorant son of a gun.

# Lullaby

A lullaby is a poem,
Laced together with care and love.
A gentle comforting place
that's warmed from the heavens above.

My children are my lullaby,
a place my heart likes to go.
Where my mind is delicately set at ease,
my soul set aglow.

They make my heart smile
with every endearing thought.
The happiness they bring to me
is worth more than I've ever bought.

To my children if you're reading this…
I want you to always know,
God knew what I needed before I did
those many years ago.

# Her man

He never wears cologne
but she knows his scent…
Its blanketed in his pillow throughout the night
and every morning she breathes it in deep
before she leaves the bed.

# Phoenix

I forgot who I was…
Don't worry I'm back.
Forced to be reborn
to learn what I lack.

I allowed you to burn me,
as I lay in the cinder.
Broken and bruised…
My pride hindered.

I emerged from the ashes
vibrant and fresh.
Lessons I've paid for
with a pound of my flesh.

I am much stronger now
then ever before,
my faith in my own wings,
they lift me to soar.

I am confident in who I am,
no longer will I be caged.
There's no way to hold me back;
No way to imprison this rage.

Goodbye to the girl
who was innocent and young…
Hello to this mean bitch
who never bites her tongue.

# Hypnotic

She's a beautiful young spirit
with an antique mind.
Crystal clear vision
with a heart that is kind.

She makes life seem effortless…
Floating away on a breeze.
You could wish to unlock her heart,
if only you had the keys.

# I need a sinner

The devil came for a visit...
On my porch, he patiently waits.
Carefully he knocked on my door,
as if at heaven's gate.

He said he's looking for a sinner,
a soul that he could own.
To take to his mighty kingdom,
built of hellfire and brimstone.

I made a deal with the devil
to free my very own soul...
He could have yours instead,
it's nothing but rot and coal.

When my lips formed your name,
a sly smile the devil did make.
He said, "Oh, that's a good one...
An easy soul to take."

As I lay comfy in bed that night
thinking of what I had done.
I didn't have an ounce of guilt...
not a single one.

N SCONE

# The cost of time

The hands on the clock move slowly,
draining my energy away.
I cannot wait till 4 o'clock
when it's time to end the work day.

Each dollar I make is shares of my life
I've been forced to bargain away.
I hope I have plenty of time to barter;
At night, this is what I pray.

If you break it down by hour,
how very little my time is worth.
I've spent 2,400 minutes this week
of the time that I'm on this earth.

I bought a pack of gum today
and think of what it cost.
I had to work 7 minutes
for that gum that I just tossed.

The hours, minutes, days and weeks
I've spent away from my loves.
Just to be able to provide my family
with socks, shoes and gloves.

The 40 hours I've spent
at work sitting at my desk,
I could have been playing with my kids
and giving my soul a rest.

# All eyes on her

She sat in the high burgundy chair,
in her most beautiful Sunday best.
Hair in perfect place,
A brooch upon her breast.

The pallbearers come upon the hill
and unbreakable as she may seem;
She wanted to crumble to the grassy floor,
staining her dress of cream.

She knew she must be strong,
for her children are standing by.
Not a mourner has seen her salty tears,
nor will she allow herself to cry.

She's the backbone and the anchor.
She'll lead this family on.
She'll save her tears for another time,
when she melts away at dawn.

On the outside she was cordial,
as though hosting a big soiree.
On the inside she wept for her husband,
the grief too heavy to weigh.

Once everyone had left her side
and she could finally be alone.
She walked through the emptiness
of what was once their loving home.

Though she may feel broken
and her heart now beats in the past.
She sacredly holds on to his memory,
that makes their undying love last.

# Enigma

Trust is an enigma
that floats lightly on the passing clouds.
It sets its sights on forward
and not dare does it make a sound.

The cloud does rain time and again
releasing its heavy depression.
The sun soon to be seen after its anguish,
to claim the cloud's confession.

Must mercy be taken
on the cloud's thunderous scorned delight;
Or may he suffer for his sins
once the moon unfolds the sky to night?

# Essence of a storm

The night is dark and windy,
the smell of rain is in the air.
The sky preparing to release its temper
without a single care.

The wind whips against the trees,
breaking limbs in its path.
Their roots have them chained in place,
victims to its wrath.

A startled cry heard from a passerby,
as the sky magically caught fire.
An electric whip made her heart skip,
as the heavens lit with hell fire.

Approaching from everywhere,
the thunderous growls do scare.
A mammoth storm is coming,
you can sense it in the air.

Thick black clouds pregnant with tears
become heavy with sorrow.
Without a sound come pouring down,
all will be fine tomorrow.

# White knight

I'm alive but I am burning,
this eternal hell within.
Bright blaze charred my beating heart,
a macabre melody on violin.

My arm outstretched for rescue;
Though flames stood in their place.
Set me free from the chains that bind me.
Violent tears stream down my face.

Will I find my knight dressed in white,
to save me from my unforgiving self?
Untangle me from my own inferno
even though he burns himself.

www.ingramcontent.com/pod-product-compliance
Lightning Source LLC
LaVergne TN
LVHW091553060526
838200LV00036B/819